CANONS OF THE COUNCIL OF LONDON
(960 AD)

Edgar,
King of the English

Translated by: D.P. Curtin

Copyright @ 2023 Dalcassian Publishing Company

All rights reserved. No part of this publication may be reproduced, distributed, or transmitted in any form or by any means, including photocopying, recording, or other electronic or mechanical methods, without the prior written permission of the publisher, except in the case of brief quotations embodied in critical reviews and certain other non-commercial uses permitted by copyright law. For permission request, write to Dalcassian Publishing Company at dalcassianpublishing at gmail.com

ISBN: 979-8-8692-1087-6 (Paperback)

Library of Congress Control Number:
Author: Curtin, D.P. (1985-)

Printed by Ingram Content Group, 1 Ingram Blvd, La Vergne, Tennessee

First printing edition 2023.

THESE CANONS WERE ISSUED BY KING EDGAR

I. We teach that God's ministers should be devoutly serving God, and ministering, and interceding for all the Christian people, and that all of them should be faithful and obedient to their elders, and that all should be promoted in common need, and that each should be a help and a helper to others both before God , than before men, and that they may be faithful and true even to their worldly masters.

CANONS OF THE COUNCIL OF LONDON

II. Let us also teach that each one should respect the other, and that the younger should carefully listen to and love their elders, and that the older should carefully teach their younger ones.

III. We also teach that they should go to every synod and have books and clothes for ecclesiastical service every year, and ink and parchment for their constitutions, and three days' supply.

IV. We also teach that every priest (going to the synod) should have his own cleric and a suitable person as a minister, and not some unknown person who loves foolishness, but that all should go in order and in the fear of God Almighty.

V. We also teach that every priest should declare in the synod if anything harms him, and if someone does him a great injury; and then let them all accept as if it had been done for them all, and help to compensate, as the bishop has noted.

VI. We also teach that every priest should declare in the synod if he knows of anyone in his parish who is disobedient to God, or who has fallen badly into mortal sin, whom he is unable to incline to amends, or does not dare to for the sake of seculars.

VII. We also teach that no business between priests should be referred to a secular judgment, but that their own associates should settle and pacify (it), or transfer it to the bishop if need be.

VIII. We also teach that no priest should voluntarily leave the church to which he was consecrated, but should have her as his legitimate spouse.

IX. We also teach that no priest should do any of those things that refer to others; not in his church, nor in his parish, nor in his society, nor in any of those things that pertain to him.

X. We also teach that no priest should receive another scholar without the forgiveness of the one whom he previously followed.

XI. We also teach that every priest, for the sake of increasing his knowledge, should carefully study the work.

XII. We also teach that a learned priest should not insult a half-learned person, but should correct him if he knows better.

XIII We also teach that no priest born in an illustrious place should despise a priest of inferior condition; if one contemplates this aright, he will (find) that all men are of the same birth.

XIV. We also teach that every priest should behave decently, and not be an unjust buyer, nor a greedy merchant.

XV. We also teach that every priest performs baptism as soon as it is required; and then in his parish he should order that every infant be baptized within 37 days; and that no one delay too long to be confirmed by the bishop.

XVI. We also teach that every priest should diligently promote Christianity, and completely extinguish all gentiles, and forbid the worship of fountains, and necromancy, and auguries, and incantations, and the divine worship of man, and obscenities, which are practiced in various prestiges, and in tediums, and in by sorceries, and in ulna, and also in various trees, and in stones, and in many other phantasms, by which many of those who ought not are deceived.

XVII. We also teach that every Christian should carefully accustom his child to Christianity, and teach him the Our Father and the Creed.

XVIII. We also teach that on the days of the feasts profane songs and diabolical games should cease.

XIX. We also teach that on Sundays the trade and assembly of the people should cease.

XX. Let us also teach that false and foolish conversations and shameful haircuts should cease.

XXI. Let us also teach that concubinage should cease, and just marriages should be loved.

XXII. We also teach that everyone should learn the Our Father and the Creed if he ever wants to lie in a consecrated cemetery or to receive the sacred Eucharist; for the reason that he is not a good Christian who does not want to learn this, nor can he legally remove others from baptism, nor receive the bishop's hand (in Confirmation) unless he first learns this.

XXIII. We also teach that there should be absolutely no conflict between anyone on holidays and fasting days

XXIV. We also teach that on feast days and fasting days oaths and ordinances are omitted.

XXV. We also teach that every man should abstain from his wife on feast days and on regular fasts.

XXVI. We also teach that the priests keep the churches with all reverence for the ecclesiastical service, and for pure service, and for no other things; let there be nothing useless there, nor in the prey; no vain conversation, no vain actions, no unseemly comportment, nor any other vanity, nor any dog come within the fence of the church, nor pigs more than one can control.

XXVII. We also teach that nothing should be stored in the church that is inappropriate there.

XXVIII. We also teach that (everyone) should be very sober in church settings, and pray diligently, and not use cups or anything useless there.

XXIX. We also teach that no one should be buried in the church unless it is known that he was well pleased with God in life, so that it may be judged from this that he is worthy of burial.

XXX. We also teach that a priest should not celebrate mass in any house, except in consecrated churches, except in case of extreme illness.

XXXI. We also teach that the priest should never celebrate mass except on a consecrated altar.

XXXII. We also teach that the priest should never celebrate mass without a book, and that the canon should be placed before his eyes, if he wishes, so that he may not touch it.

XXXIII. We also teach that every priest should have a corporal vestment when he celebrates mass, and a vest under his white robe, and that all vestments for mass should be properly woven.

XXXIV. We also teach that every priest should take care to have a good and at least a just book.

XXXV. We also teach that no priest should celebrate mass alone unless he has someone to answer for him.

XXXVI. We also teach that every priest should receive the Eucharist fasting, except in case of extreme illness.

XXXVII. We also teach that no priest should celebrate high mass more than three times in one day.

XXXVIII. We also teach that the priest should always have the Eucharist ready, as needed, and that he should carefully keep it in purity, and be careful that it does not become stale; He will make amends, who neglected this.

XXXIX. We also teach that a priest should never presume to celebrate mass unless he has everything that pertains to the Holy Eucharist, that is, a pure offering, and pure wine, and pure water. Woe to him who begins mass before he has all these things! And woe to him who adds to them what is impure! This would be similar to what the Jews did, when they mixed vinegar and gall together, and afterwards handed it to Christ in mockery.

XL. We also teach that a priest is never worthy to celebrate Mass who does not himself perceive the Holy Eucharist; and what is consecrated is never consecrated again.

XLI. We also teach that every chalice in which the Holy Eucharist is secreted must be molten, and never secreted in a wooden one.

XLII. We also teach that everything that approaches the altar and belongs to the church should be very pure and decently arranged, and nothing (impure) should approach it, but should be placed in the sanctuary in a very honorable way, and that a light should always burn in the church when mass is sung.

XLIII. We also teach that nothing consecrated should be neglected, neither consecrated water, nor salt, nor frankincense, nor bread, nor anything holy.

XLIV. We also teach that no wife should approach the altar while mass is being celebrated.

CANONS OF THE COUNCIL OF LONDON

XLV. We also teach that at the appointed time the bell should be rung, and every priest should sing his appointed song in the church, and there he should pray earnestly with the fear of God, and intercede for all the people.

XLVI. We also teach that a secular or conventual priest should not come inside the door of the church, nor inside the sanctuary, without his fur coat, nor at least to the altar, to minister there without that vestment.

XLVII. We also teach that no holy initiated man should conceal his haircut, nor allow it to be cut badly, nor grow his beard for a certain time, if he wishes to have the blessing of God, and of St. Peter, and ours.

XLVIII. We also teach that all the priests should be of one mind on feast days and fasts, and that they should all pray in one way, lest they lead the people into error.

XLIX. We also teach that every fast is to be honored by almsgiving, that is, that whoever, out of devotion to God, wishes diligently to give alms, then his fasting is more acceptable to God.

L. We also teach that the priests should all work together in the ministries of the church, and that the salary should be equal in the space of a year in all the ministries of the church.

LI. Let us also teach that priests should diligently teach the youth, and draw them to work, so that they may have the help of the Church.

LII. We also teach that the priests should preach to the people every Sunday, and always set a good example for them.

LIII. We also teach that no Christian should eat blood of any kind.

LIV. We also teach that the priests should remind the people of what they must diligently do to God, that they may be just in paying tithes and other things, first to the plow alms 15 days from Easter, and tithes of the offspring to Pentecost, and the crops of the land to the feast of all saints, and the denarius of St. Peter at the feast of Peter, and the census of the church at the feast of Martin.

LV. We also teach that the priests should distribute the alms of the people in such a way as to make God propitious to them as well as to accustom the people to alms.

LVI. We also teach that the priests should sing psalms when they distribute alms, and that the poor should diligently pray for them to intercede diligently for the people.

LVII. We also teach that priests should guard themselves against drunkenness, and forbid it to other people by carefully reproving it.

LVIII. We also teach that no priest should be a brewer, nor in any way act as a clown with himself by himself, or by others; but let him, as befits his order, be prudent and venerable.

LIX. We also teach that priests should be careful not to swear to themselves, and even strongly forbid it.

LX. We also teach that no priest should love the company of women too much, but should love his legitimate wife, that is, his Church.

LXI. We also teach that no priest should bear false witness, nor be a thief from counsels.

LXII. We also teach that the priest should never visit ordeals or take oaths.

LXIII. We also teach that a priest should not swear against a thane in the purgatory, unless the thane has sworn before him.

LXIV. We also teach that the priest should not be a hunter, nor a hawker, nor a drinker, but should lean on his books, as befits his order.

LXV. We also teach that every priest should teach confession and penance to him who confesses to himself, and also help him to make amends, and provide the sick with the Holy Eucharist when he needs it, and anoint him also, if he desires this, and wrap him carefully after death; and let nothing vain be allowed about the body, but let it be decently buried with the fear of God.

LXVI. We also teach that every priest should have oil both for baptism and for anointing the sick; let him also be ready to diligently promote the rights of the people and Christianity in every way, both by preaching well and by setting a good example; then Almighty God will bestow upon him that which will be most acceptable to him.

LXVII. We also teach that every priest knows how to answer, when he takes away his chrism, what he has done in the prayers for the king and the bishop.

CONFESSION

I. When a man wishes to make a confession of his sins, he acts manfully, and is not ashamed to confess his crimes and misdeeds by accusing himself; because from this comes forgiveness, and because without confession there is no forgiveness. For confession heals, confession justifies.

Please, Lord, let your mercy prevent this servant of yours, so that all his iniquities may be wiped out by the speedy indulgence of Jesus Christ our Lord.

Hear, please, Lord, the supplicant prayers of those who cry out to you, please, Lord.

II. Whoever is a physician of men's souls and knows their actions, let him study division and discrimination, how to enjoin repentance from men's actions; yet he will not condemn them, nor cause them to despair. When a man wants to confess his offenses to him, let him first listen patiently, how wise his intention is; if he is willing and able to humbly confess his actions, and you perceive that he repents of his sins, teach him lovingly and with mercy. If he cannot confess his actions and examine his liabilities,

III. Ask him about his character, and extort his guilt, and explain his actions, and think that you should never judge in the same way the rich and the poor, the free and the slaves, the old and the young, the healthy and the infirm, the humble and the proud, the strong and the weak, the sacred initiates and the laity.

Every deed a prudent judge must discern prudently, when it was done, and where, or when; at no time is unjust permitted, but let one guard against it as carefully as possible on feast days and fasts and in festive places. And the more powerful and of greater rank a man is, the more seriously he must correct the injustice before God and before the world, since the powerful and the powerless cannot have equal burdens, nor can the weak be like the firm; These, then, are to be distinguished and to be distinguished discreetly.

IV. From now on he should rise humbly to his confessor and say first: I believe in the Lord, the supreme Father, the ruler of all things, and in the Son, and in the Holy Spirit; and I believe that I live after death; and I believe that I will rise again on the day of judgment, and I believe that I deserve all this through the power of God and his mercy.

V. And then, with a contrite and humble heart, he should say his confession to his confessor, bowing humbly, and say thus:

> *I confess to Almighty God, and to my confessor, the spiritual healer, all my sins, by which I have ever been polluted by the malignity of the spirit, whether in deeds or in thoughts, whether with men, or with women, or with any creature, natural or supernatural sins.*

VI. I confess that I have a gastrimargia of food both in the morning and in the evening. I confess all covetousness, and envy, and self-loathing, and tongue-twisting vice, falsehood, and unjust glory, and vanity, and unjust magnificence, and all pride, which happens to the wrong counsel of my body. I confess that I have too often been the author of sin, and the supporter of sin, and the connoisseur of sin, and the teacher of sin.

VII. I confess the murder of my soul, and perjury, and sedition, and pride, disregarding the commandment of God. I confess all that I have ever seen with my eyes for covetousness or for taking away, or heard with my ears for useless things, or have spoken with my mouth in vain.

VIII. I confess all the sins of my body, skin, and flesh, and bones, and nerves, and kidneys, and cartilages, and tongue, and lips, and throat, and teeth, and hair, and marrow, and everything soft or hard, wet or dry. I confess that I kept my baptism worse than I promised my Lord, and I did not keep my order, which I ought to keep for the love of God and his saints, and for my own eternal salvation. I confess that I had often neglected my canonical hours, and had offended the souls of my masters, and had taken my Lord's name in vain.

IX. I ask the forgiveness of all (sins) from my Lord, that the devil may never lie in wait for me, that I may not die without confession and correction of my sins, just as today I confess all my offenses before the Lord, the Savior Christ, who governs heaven and earth, and before this holy altar, and with these relics, and before my confessor, and the Lord's priest, and I am in a pure and true confession, and in a good will to make amends for all my sins, and then to abstain in such a way as I ever can.

X. And you, Savior Christ, be merciful to my soul, and forgive and erase my sins and my debts, which I committed once or ever before, and lead me to your highest kingdom, and there I will dwell with your saints and elect without end in eternal I humbly beseech you, priest of the Lord, to be my witness on the day of judgment, so that the devil may not have power over me. and that you may be my advocate with the Lord, that I may atone for my sins and my liabilities, and abstain from others of this kind: for this the Lord, who lives and reigns forever, will help me. Amen.

THE METHOD OF IMPOSING PENITENCE.

I. The old and the young, the rich and the poor, the healthy and the infirm, and of whatever rank, and if any one sins unwillingly, let him not be like him who sinned willingly and voluntarily; and if any one transgresses even under necessity, let him always be worthy of the protection and correction of the law, because he was compelled by necessity to do what he committed.

II. Every deed must be carefully distinguished before God and before the world.

These rites are observed on the other side of the sea, namely:

III. That every bishop should be in his episcopal seat on Wednesday, which we call the head of the fast; then let any one of them who is defiled by mortal sins come to him in that province on that day, and confess his sins to him, and let him then teach him penance, according to the reason of every guilt; who, if he be of great enormity, should be removed from ecclesiastical communion, yet he should be urged to his own need, and be admonished;

IV. And thenceforth, on the Thursday before Easter, all shall gather to their respective places, and the bishop shall sing over him, and give absolution; and he should return home afterwards with the blessing of the bishop: this is to be observed by all the Christian people.

V. However, the priest must carefully consider with what contrition and with what perfection he has compensated for the penance that was imposed on him, and how he should grant himself remission.

VI. If a layman kills another without cause, he fasts for 7 years, 3 on bread and water, 4, as the confessor taught him, and after seven years he makes up for it; afterwards let him carefully mourn his crime, with what energy he can, since it is unknown how his repentance will be received with God.

VII. If a man wishes to kill another, and is unable to fulfill his wish, he must fast for three years, one on bread and water, and two, as his confessor taught him.

VIII. If a layman unwillingly kills someone, he fasts for three years; one bread and water, and two as his confessor taught him, and let him always mourn his crime.

IX. If he is a subdeacon, he fasts for six years. If he is a deacon, he fasts seven years. If he is a priest, he fasts ten years, and a bishop twelve, and mourns always.

X. If a man kills his child unwillingly, he must fast for five years, three on bread and water, as above.

XI. If a bishop or a priest kills any one, he shall lose his order, and afterwards he shall carefully compensate.

XII. If a wife kills her child within herself, or after it is born, by drink or other things, she shall fast for ten years, three on bread and water, and seven as her confessor has sanctioned for her out of mercy, and then mourn for it.

XIII If a man kills his servant without guilt in his rage, he shall fast for three years.

XIV. If a woman beats her husband out of some jealousy, and he dies as a result, and he is innocent, she fasts for seven years, and if he is guilty, she fasts for three years, and mourns her beloved forever.

XV. If a man kills himself voluntarily by arms, or by some instigation of the devil, it is not permitted that masses be sung for such a person, nor that the body be carried to the earth with the singing of any psalm, nor that it be buried in a pure burial. The same judgment is to be made to him who, for his guilt, ends his life with tortures, such as are the thief, the murderer, and the traitor to his master.

XVI. If a man defiles himself with an animal, or a male with another, if he is 20 years old, he shall fast for fifteen years; and if a man has his wife, and he himself is 40 years old, and commits such a thing, let him abstain and fast as long as he lives, and do not presume to perceive the Lord's body before death takes him away. He who commits such a thing, being young and ignorant, shall be severely beaten.

XVII. If a person commits adultery, he must fast for seven years three days a week on bread and water, whether he is the wife or the husband.

XVIII. If a man deserts his spouse, and marries another wife, commits adultery, he shall not be granted any of the rights which belong to Christians, neither dead nor alive, nor shall he be buried here with Christians. And the same should be done to the wife. And of the relatives who have done the same, each one shall lose his right, unless they are willing to return quickly and diligently make amends.

XIX. If a man has a wife and also a concubine, no priest shall render him any service with the Christians, unless he returns to amends, and keeps one for himself, either wife or concubine.

XX. If a man cohabits with the legitimate wife of another, or a wife with the legitimate spouse of another wife, he must fast for seven years, three on bread and water, and four as the confessor has taught him, and he must always mourn his crime.

XXI If any wife marries two brothers, one after the other, they are subject to judgment, and they must be diligent in penitence as long as they live, as their confessor taught them; and at their death the priest should perform the duty for them, as is done for Christians, if they have promised that they wished to make better amends, if they had lived longer.

XXII. If a man continues in any nefarious association of sin, he shall end his life without any repentance; we do not know of any counsel to supply him, except that this belongs to the judgment of God, and cannot be absolved.

XXIII. If any wife be betrothed, it shall not be permitted for any other man to redeem her for him; if anyone does this, let him be excommunicated.

XXIV. If any man by fraud abducts his wife, or an uninvited virgin, for unlawful intercourse, let him be excommunicated.

XXV. If a man by his enticements seduces another man away from him for the sake of fornication and cohabits with her unwillingly; if a man is a sacred initiate, he loses his order; if he is a layman, let him be excommunicated from all Christian offices.

XXVI. If a virgin is betrothed, and during this interval she is abducted, or is taken away under some pretext from the man to whom she was betrothed, and then it happens that she comes into his sight, when he can be forgiven, because she was absent from him against her will.

XXVII. If a woman is consecrated, and then returns to worldly vanity, and rears a family, and thinks that by her possessions she will make amends for what she has turned away from God, this is nothing; but let him leave the association of sin, and return to Christ, and live his life as his confessor had taught him, and then most diligently correct the offense.

XXVIII. If a priest or a monk kills a man, he loses his order and fasts for ten years; five bread and water, and five three days a week; and the rest let him enjoy his food, and always mourn his crime.

> *For the deacon eight bread and water, and for the rest as above.*

> *Cleric 4 years; 6 bread and water.*

> *Layman 5 years; 3 bread and water, as above.*

XXIX. If anyone slays a sacred initiate, or his own nearest relative, let him leave his land and possessions, and do as the pope instructs him, and let him mourn always.

XXX. If a priest or a monk practices lascivious intercourse, or violates marriage, he must fast for 10 years and mourn forever. Deacon 7, cleric 6, layman 5 [years] as a result of murder.

XXXI. If a priest or a monk or a deacon has a legitimate wife, before he is consecrated, he leaves her and receives orders, and afterwards receives her often because of cohabitation, each of them shall fast as if for murder, and they shall mourn greatly.

XXXII. If a priest, or a monk, or a deacon, or a layman, or a cleric, joins a nun, each one shall fast, according to his order, as if for murder, and shall always abstain from meat; and a nun for ten years, as also a priest, and let them mourn always.

XXXIII. If a man wishes to have intercourse with a nun, and she refuses, he must fast for one year on bread and water for that unjust desire. If a man wishes to have intercourse with another's legitimate wife, and she does not wish to do so, he must fast for one year on bread and water for that unjust wish.

XXXIV. If a man wishes to have intercourse with the lawful wife of another, and she is unwilling, he fasts three Lent days on bread and water, one in summer, another in autumn, and a third in winter.

XXXV. If a man wishes to marry his wife unjustly, he must fast 40 days on bread and water.

XXXVI. If anyone finds another with his daughter, he shall make amends with [the girl's] friends, and each shall fast for one year on Wednesdays and Fridays as long as he lives, and shall always mourn his crime.

XXXVII. If anyone has intercourse with an animal, he must fast for 15 years; eight bread and water, and seven others every year on the three days of Lent, and on Wednesdays and Fridays, as long as he lives, and let him always mourn his crime.

XXXVIII. If anyone pollutes himself from his own will, he must fast for three years; every three days of Lent bread and water, and let him abstain from meat every day, except Sunday.

XXXIX. If a man kills another by poisoning, he shall fast for seven years, three with bread and water, and for another four years with bread and water three days a week; and may he mourn always.

XL. If any one pierces a man with a pin, he shall fast for three years; one bread and water, and two three days a week bread and water; and if a man dies because of that pin, then he fasts for seven years; as it is written here, and let him always mourn his crime.

XLI. If a person uses witchcraft to (win) the love of another and gives it to him in food or drink or in the art of enchantment, if he is a layman, he fasts for half a year on Wednesdays and Fridays on bread and water, and on other days he uses his own food. except the flesh. A clerk for one year, as above, bread and water three days a week. Deacon three years, as above. A priest for five years; one of them bread and water, and four on every Friday bread and water, and on other days he should abstain from meat.

XLII. If any one, in supernatural matters, has defiled himself by any act against God's creature, let him mourn always as long as he lives, according to what has happened.

XLIII. If a man crushes his child in his sleep, so that it may die, he shall fast for three years; one bread and water, and two years three days a week; and if it was done through drunkenness, let him compensate more severely, as his confessor taught, and let him always mourn it.

XLIV. If a weak ethnic infant dies (that is, without baptism), and this is due to the procrastination of the priest, let him lose his order, and diligently correct this; and if this be done through the negligence of their friends, they shall fast for three years, one on bread and water, and two years on three days a week, and mourn this always.

XLV. If anyone sells a Christian to ethnicism, he is not worthy of any peace with the Christians, unless he himself then buys back the house which he had previously sold abroad; and if he is unable to do this, let him divide the whole price, by the grace of God, and buy another at a different price, and then let him go, and add to this the compensation for three whole years, as the confessor taught him. And if he has not the money with which he could redeem the man, he shall compensate more severely, that is, for seven whole years, and he shall mourn always.

XLVI. If a person greatly weakens himself by many sins, and then he wishes to abstain from them and diligently correct himself, he must incline to a monastery and serve there always to God and men, as he is taught, or he must go abroad far from his country, and do penance always as long as he lives, and obtain salvation let him seek for his soul at least on earth by the most severe compensation that he can ever experience, as it is taught.

CONCERNING REPENTANCE

I. In this confession, the necessary help of any theologian is very helpful, just as a good physician is the healer of a sick man.

II. Man often sins through concupiscence, and not infrequently through the instigation of the devil; and this is terrible, that the sacred initiates sin so grievously with God that they lose their order.

III. And for this to be corrected we need rigid penance, always according to order and according to the manner of sin, according to the canonical laws. And we must also inquire about man's strength, and about his mode of [satisfaction], and about the remorse of the soul itself. Some do penance for a year; some more than a year; and then, according to the offense, some should repent for a month, some for a month longer; some repent a week, some more a week; some repent for a day, and some for more days, and some all the days of their lives.

IV. If a physician is to take good care of serious wounds, he must use good medicines; There are no wounds so bad as the wounds of sin, because by them man deserves eternal death, unless he is healed by confession, abstinence, and penance.

V. Then the physician must be wise and prudent, who must take care of the wounds. He must first be cured by good teaching, and by doing this the poison that is in him will be purged, that is, he must first purge himself by confession.

VI. Every man must vomit out his sins by good doctrine and confession, in the same way as a fatal disease is done by a good drink.

VII. No physician can treat well before the poison has passed, nor can any man even teach penance well to one who does not want to confess, nor can any man correct sins without confession; just as he who has consumed something lethal can be less well cared for, unless he vomits the poison altogether.

VIII. After confession, through penance, one can quickly earn the mercy of God, if he laments with his inner heart and mourns that he was previously led to injustice by the instigation of the devil.

IX. A prudent penitence is also very fitting for a prudent confessor, just as it is absolutely necessary for a good physician to take care of a sick person. The compensation of the necessary use and of the works of man must be inquired into according to the canonical laws, and the reason of the statute also for the forces, and for the manner, and for him who recognizes the mourning and anxiety of his own heart

X. It is a serious penance that a layman lays down his arms, and wanders far away with bare feet, and does not spend the night anywhere, and fasts and is very watchful, and prays diligently day and night, and willingly tires himself, and is so uncultivated that neither iron nor hair nor touch the nails.

XI. Neither let him enter the baths, nor a soft bed, nor taste flesh, nor any of it from which he can be drunk; let him not enter the churches, but let him diligently seek the holy place, and confess his guilt, and ask for intercession; and let him not kiss anyone, but always mourn his sins very much.

XII. He acts cruelly who condemns himself in this way, yet happy is he, if he watches over no other thing than to fully correct (sins); since no man in the world offends God so much by sins, that he cannot make amends with God, if he diligently approaches this.

XIII Penances are made in various ways, and many people can redeem (it) with alms.

XIV. If anyone has the means for this, let him erect a church to the praise of God; and if he is able in addition, let him add land and admit ten juniors, who may serve there for him, and there be able to minister to God every day; and he should also establish the church of God everywhere according to his ability, and he should establish public roads by deepening bridges over the waters, and over muddy roads, and he should distribute, for God's sake, diligently what he has according to the proportion of his abilities, and he should diligently help the poor, widows, and orphans, and strangers ; let him hand over his own slaves, and redeem from other men the freedom of his slaves, and at least the poor who have been devastated by war, and feed the needy, and clothe them with lodgings, and provide them with a hearth, a bath, and a bed, and for his own need he shall diligently intercede everywhere in the masses and with the songs of psalms, and from devotion to his Lord he will punish himself as severely as possible by abstinence from food and drink, and from any bodily lust.

XV. And if any one has less resources, let him diligently do what he can according to his strength; tithe all that he has in the fear of God, and examine himself as often as he can opportunely, and often visit the churches with his alms, and sanctify the place where candles are lit with salutations, and grant shelter, and food, and protection to those who need them, and fire and sustenance. and bed and bath, and cause the poor to be clothed and helped as much as he can.

XVI. Out of love for God he visits the sick in heart, and the sick, and buries the dead out of devotion to God; and often And if a man has still less means, let him diligently do whatever he can for his strength, at least by laboring his body against lust. If before by soft lust he pleased the devil, now he fasts, on the contrary, because he had done it before by unjust indolence; let him watch and labor, on the contrary, because before he was often drowsy and lazy, when he should not have been, or used too much uselessly; let him endure the cold and the cold bath against the heat, which by his desire he has everywhere aroused. And if he has provoked any one unjustly at any place, let him compensate diligently; and if anyone offends him, he willingly remits it from the fear of God, and always, as far as he can, thinks very carefully what he can do instead of compensation against the individual sins which were brought up before by the seed of the devil. and if he has led anyone astray in order to gain anything, let him carefully guide him afterwards into the right way. This is what I want; if he has incited someone to sin, let him do as is necessary, lead him thence, and lead him on the right path, and carefully exhort everyone from sins; then immediately his sins will be lighter.

XVII. The same judgment can be judged by anyone with the counsel of the confessor, who constantly abstains from his sins and wants to correct his sins, distributes out of devotion to God all that he has, and with them abandons the whole earth and country, and all the love of the world, and serves the Lord day and night, and labor as much as he can against his own desire all the days of his life. What more can he do than to exhort (for his own advantage) every man to the right as diligently as he can.

Here is how the patient should redeem his fast.

XVIII. One day's fasting can be redeemed with one penny: any man can redeem one day's fasting with two hundred and twenty psalms; any man can redeem 12 months of fasting for 30 solids, or if he frees someone (from prison) who is valued at that value. And instead of fasting for one day, let him sing six times: Beati immaculate. and the Our Father six times, and for one day's fasting, to bend the knees, and bow 60 times to the ground with the Our Father. A person can also redeem the fast of one day, if he stretches out all his limbs to God in his prayers, and with true contrition, and with right faith, and sings 15 times Have mercy on me, God, and 15 times Our Father. And then let him rather be granted the remission of sins for the day.

XIX. Anyone can make up for a seven-year fast in 12 months if he ends every day by singing psalms on the psaltery, and the same at night and in the evening. It can also be redeemed by a single mass of 12 days of fasting; and by ten masses a 4-month fast can be alleviated, and by 30 masses a 12-month fast can be alleviated, if he wishes to intercede for himself out of the true love of God, and to confess his sins to his confessor, and to correct them, as he has taught him, and diligently always from to abstain from them.

Of the magnates.

I. Thus, a powerful man and rich in friends can greatly alleviate his penance with the help of his friends. First, in the name of God, through the testimony of his confessor, let him show his true faith, and forgive all those who have sinned against him, and make his confession fearlessly, and promise abstinence, and accept penance with much groaning.

II. Then he lays down his arms and the empty worship of his clothes, and takes a staff in his hand, and goes diligently with bare feet, and puts on his body woolen clothes, or coats, and does not enter the bed, but lies on the floor, and does so as the number of 7 years within three days to be moderated; first, let him take 12 men to help him, and fast for three days on bread and green vegetables, and water, and to complete it, in whatever way he can, he must procure for himself seven times 120 men, who shall each fast for him for three days; then they fast as many fasts as there are days in 7 years.

III. When a person fasts, let him distribute the dishes which he ought to use to all the poor of God, and for the three days during which he fasts, neglect the affairs of the world, and spend the day and night as often as he can in the churches, and there watch carefully with the alms-light, and cry to God , and he asks for forgiveness with a groaning heart, and often bends his knees over the sign of the cross; sometimes he raises himself up, sometimes he prostrates himself, and a mighty man carefully knows how to shed tears and to blow away sins. And for three days he feeds the poor as much as he can, and on the fourth day he washes them all, and receives hospitality, and gives money, and he himself is doing penance about washing their feet (busy), and masses are said that day for him as many as can ever be obtained, and At the time of those masses, absolution is given to him, and then he receives the Holy Eucharist, unless the sinner is too serious, so that he is still unable to (perceive it). as energetically as he ever can, he must hold to what is just, and completely cast off all gentilism, diligently correct his mind and manners, words and deeds, worship all justice, and avoid injustice by the help of God, as diligently as he ever can. And he who has done what he promised God will do to his greatest advantage.

IV. This is the relief of the rich penitence of a powerful man and friends; but the weak cannot proceed in this way but must seek it more carefully within himself. And this is also the most fair thing, that each one should take revenge on himself for his own offenses by careful correction. »

ECCLESIASTICAL LAWS OF KING EDGAR.

This is the institution which Eadgar established with the counsel of his wise men for the glory of God, and for himself a royal dignity, and for the benefit of all his people.

I. On the immunity of the church, and the debts to be paid to it.

Let this be the first thing that the churches of God are worthy of their right, and all tithes are given to the primary church to which the parish belongs; and then it is presented either from the land of the thani, or from the land of the peasants, as it is brought round by the plough.

II. Of the ecclesiastical census.

If there is any one of the thanes who has a church in his fee, in which there is a cemetery, he shall then give a third part of his proper tithes to his church. If any one has a church in which there is no cemetery, then out of nine parts he shall give whatever he wants to his priest, and any ecclesiastical census shall pass to the primary church from any free land.

III. Of tithes.

And each tithe of the fruits is presented at Pentecost, and of the crops of the earth at the equinox. And any ecclesiastical census shall be presented at the feast of Martin, by a full fine, any judicial record. And if anyone does not want to pay the tithe, as we have said, let him go to him. The prefect of the king, and the bishop, and the presbyter of the church, and they take, against his will, the tenth part which belongs to the church, and they assign to him the ninth part, and the eight parts are divided into two, and the lord takes half, the bishop half, whether it be the king's or the thane's minister.

IV. About the money put into each house.

And every coin deposited in individual houses shall be given on the day of the feast of Peter, and whoever has not paid by that term shall take it to Rome, and 30 other denarii besides, and bring back from thence a certificate that he has delivered so many there. And then returning home, he shall pay the king 120 solidi, and if he does not want to pay him again, he shall then carry him to Rome, and compensate him with something similar, and then returning home, he shall pay the king two hundred solidi. If he refuses to pay the third time, he will lose all that he has.

V. On feast days and fasts.

Every festival of the day of the sun shall be celebrated from the hour of the afternoon of the day of Saturday, until the dawn of the day of the moon, under the fines which the book of justice records; and every other festival day (be celebrated) as is just. And the appointed fast shall be observed with all devotion.

LATIN TEXT

Canones editi sub Edgardo rege

I. Docemus ut Dei ministri sint devote Deo servientes, et ministrantes, et pro omni populo Christiano intercedentes, et ut omnes illi senioribus suis sint fideles et obedientes, et omnes promoti in communi necessitate, ac ut quilibet sit aliis auxilio et adjutorio tam coram Deo, quam coram hominibus, et ut sint etiam dominis suis mundanis fidi et veri.

II. Docemus etiam, ut quilibet honoret alterum, et juniores diligenter audiant seniores suos et ament, et seniores diligenter doceant juniores suos.

III. Docemus etiam, ut illi ad quamlibet synodum (abeant et) habeant quotannis libros et vestimenta ad servitium ecclesiasticum, et atramentum ac pergamenas ad eorum constitutiones, et trium dierum commeatum.

IV. Docemus etiam, ut sacerdos quilibet ad synodum (abiens) habeat clericum suum et aptum hominem pro ministro, et non ignotum aliquem, qui stultitiam amet, sed proficiscantur omnes in ordine et in Dei omnipotentis timore.

V. Docemus etiam, ut quilibet sacerdos in synodo enuntiet, si quid ei noceat, et si aliquis magnam ipsi injuriam fecerit; et tunc illi omnes suscipiant quasi sibi omnibus factam, et adjuvent ad compensationem, prouti episcopus annotaverit.

VI. Docemus etiam, ut quilibet sacerdos in synodo enuntiet, si in parochia sua noscat aliquem erga Deum contumacem, vel qui in peccatum mortale male inciderit, quem ad emendationem inclinare nequit, vel non audet propter saeculares.

VII. Docemus etiam, ut nullum negotium, quod inter sacerdotes est, deferatur ad judicium saeculare, sed componant, ac pacificent (illud) proprii illorum socii, vel transferant ad episcopum si opus fuerit.

VIII. Docemus etiam, ut nullus presbyter sponte ecclesiam deserat, cui consecratus erat, sed habeat eam pro legitima conjuge.

IX. Docemus etiam, ut nullus sacerdos faciat aliquid eorum, quae ad alterum spectant; non in ecclesia ejus, nec in parochia ejus, neque in societate illius, neque in aliqua earum rerum quae ad eum pertinent.

X. Docemus etiam, ut nullus sacerdos suscipiat alterius scholarem absque venia ejus quem prius sequebatur.

XI. Docemus etiam ut quilibet sacerdos augendae scientiae causa diligenter discat opificium.

XII. Docemus etiam, ut quis doctus sacerdos non contumelia afficiat semidoctum, sed corrigat eum, si melius norit.

XIII. Docemus etiam, ut nullus sacerdos illustri loco natus, contemnat inferioris conditionis sacerdotem; si quis hoc recte contempletur, omnes homines ejusdem esse nativitatis (inveniet).

XIV. Docemus etiam, ut quilibet sacerdos decenter se gerat, et non sit emptor injustus, nec avarus mercator.

XV. Docemus etiam, ut quilibet sacerdos baptismum peragat, simul ac requiritur; et deinde in parochia sua praecipiat, ut quilibet infans baptizetur intra 37 dies; et ut nemo nimis diu ab episcopo confirmari differat.

XVI. Docemus etiam, ut quilibet sacerdos Christianismum diligenter promoveat, et omnem gentilismum omnino exstinguat, et prohibeat fontium adorationem, et necromantiam, et auguria, et incantationes, et divinum hominis cultum, et offacias, quae exercentur in variis prestigiis, et in tedis, et in sortilegiis, et in ulnis, et etiam in variis arboribus, et in saxis, et in multis aliis phantasmatibus, quibus multi eorum qui non deberent, decipiuntur.

XVII. Docemus etiam, ut quilibet Christianus infantem suum ad Christianismum diligenter adsuescat, et eum Pater noster et Credo doceat.

XVIII. Docemus etiam, ut diebus festis cessent profana cantica, et ludi diabolici.

XIX. Docemus etiam, ut cessent diebus Solis mercaturae et conventus populi.

XX. Docemus etiam, ut cessent falsa et stulta colloquia, et ignominiosae tonsurae.

XXI. Docemus etiam, ut cessent concubinatus, et amentur justa conjugia.

XXII. Docemus etiam, ut quilibet discat Pater noster, et Credo, si quando in consecrato coemeterio jacere vel Eucharistiam sacram percipere velit; propterea quia is non est bonus Christianus, qui hoc discere non vult, nec jure potest alios e baptismate levare, nec episcopi manum accipere (in Confirmatione) nisi hoc prius addiscat.

XXIII. Docemus etiam, ut in diebus festis et statis jejuniis nulla omnino contentio sit inter quoscunque
Homines.

XXIV. Docemus etiam, ut in diebus festis et jejuniis juramenta et ordalia praetermittantur.

XXV. Docemus etiam, ut quilibet vir abstineat ab uxore sua in diebus festis et statis jejuniis.

XXVI. Docemus etiam, ut presbyteri ecclesias custodiant cum omni veneratione ad ecclesiasticum ministerium, et ad purum servitium, et ad nullas alias res; neque sit aliquid inutile ibi, neque in vicima; non permittantur vana colloquia, nec vanae actiones, neque indecora compotatio, neque unquam alia vanitas, neque intra ecclesiae sepem canis aliquis veniat, neque porcorum plures quam quis regere possit.

XXVII. Docemus etiam, ut nihil in ecclesia reponatur, quod ibidem indecens sit.

XXVIII. Docemus etiam, ut (omnes) in ecclesiae encaeniis valde sobrii sint, et diligenter orent, nec pocula, neque aliquid inutile ibi exerceant.

XXIX. Docemus etiam, ut in ecclesia nemo sepeliatur, nisi sciatur quod in vita Deo bene placuerit, ut inde judicetur, quod sit sepultura dignus.

XXX. Docemus etiam, ut sacerdos in nulla domo missam celebret, nisi in consecratis ecclesiis, praeterquam ob extremam alicujus aegritudinem.

XXXI. Docemus etiam, ut sacerdos nunquam saltem missam celebret nisi super consecratum altare.

XXXII. Docemus etiam, ut sacerdos nunquam missam celebret absque libro, et sit canon ei ante oculos positus, si velit, ne forte impingat.

XXXIII. Docemus etiam, ut quilibet sacerdos habeat corporalem vestem, cum missam celebrat, et subuculam sub alba sua, et omnia vestimenta missae debite contexta.

XXXIV. Docemus etiam, ut quilibet sacerdos diligenter curet, ut bonum et saltem justum librum habeat.

XXXV. Docemus etiam, ut nullus sacerdos solus missam celebret, si non habeat eum qui ipsi respondeat.

XXXVI. Docemus etiam, ut quilibet sacerdos Eucharistiam accipiat jejunans, nisi ob extremam aegritudinem.

XXXVII. Docemus etiam, ut nullus sacerdos uno die saepius quam ter ad summum missam celebret.

XXXVIII. Docemus etiam, ut sacerdos semper habeat paratam Eucharistiam, prout opus fuerit, et hanc diligenter in puritate custodiat, et caveat ne inveterescat, si autem inveteraverit, ut accipi nequeat, tunc comburatur in puro igne, et cineres sub altari condantur, et diligenter apud Deum emendet, qui hoc neglexit.

XXXIX. Docemus etiam, ut sacerdos nunquam praesumat missam celebrare, nisi omnia habeat, quae ad S. Eucharistiam pertinent, hoc est puram oblationem, et vinum purum, et aquam puram. Vae illi qui missam inchoat antequam haec omnia habeat! Et vae illi qui impurum quid addit illis! hoc simile esset ei quod Judaei fecerunt, cum acetum et fel simul miscerent, et illud postea Christo in ludibrium porrigerent.

XL. Docemus etiam, quod sacerdos nunquam sit dignus missam celebrare, qui non ipse S. Eucharistiam percipit; nec consecratum unquam denuo consecretur.

XLI. Docemus etiam, ut quilibet calix fusus sit, in quo S. Eucharistia consecretur, et in ligneo nunquam consecretur.

XLII. Docemus etiam, ut omnia, quae altari appropinquant, et ad ecclesiam pertinent, sint valde pura, et digne disposita, et nihil (impurum) appropinquet illud, sed reponatur sanctuarium valde honorifice, et semper lumen ardeat in ecclesia, cum missa decantatur.

XLIII. Docemus etiam, ut non negligatur aliquid consecratum, non aqua consecrata, nec sal, nec thus, nec panis, nec aliquid sanctum.

XLIV. Docemus etiam, ut nulla uxor altare appropinquet, quandiu missa celebratur.

XLV. Docemus etiam, ut justo stato tempore campana pulsetur, et sacerdos quilibet cantum suum horarium in ecclesia psallat, et ibi cum Dei timore sedulo oret, et pro omni populo intercedat.

XLVI. Docemus etiam, ut sacerdos saecularis, vel conventualis aliquis, non veniat intra ostium ecclesiae, nec intra sacrarium, absque superpelliceo suo, neque saltem ad altare, ut ibi ministret absque vestitu illo.

XLVII. Docemus etiam, ut nullus sacris initiatus homo tonsuram suam consecret, nec eam male tonderi permittat, nec barbam suam per aliquod tempus alat, siquidem benedictionem Dei, et S. Petri, et nostram habere velit.

XLVIII. Docemus etiam, ut omnes sacerdotes festis diebus et jejuniis unanimes sint, et omnes uno modo orent, ne populum in errorem ducant.

XLIX. Docemus etiam, ut quodlibet jejunium eleemosynis honorificetur, hoc est, ut quisquis ex devotione erga Deum eleemosynam sedulo dare velit, tunc jejunium ipsius Deo sit gratius.

L. Docemus etiam, ut sacerdotes in ecclesiae ministeriis omnes simul operam navent, et sit aequale salarium in anni spatio in omnibus ecclesiae ministeriis.

LI. Docemus etiam, ut sacerdotes juventutem sedulo doceant, et ad opificia trahant, ut Ecclesiae auxilium (inde) habeant.

LII. Docemus etiam, ut sacerdotes quolibet die Solis ad populum praedicent, et semper bonum iis praebeant exemplum.

LIII. Docemus etiam, ut nullus Christianus sanguinem comedat alicujus generis.

LIV. Docemus etiam, ut sacerdotes populum admoneant ejus, quod sedulo Deo facere debent, ut justi sint in reddendis decimis et aliis rebus, primo aratri eleemosynis 15 dies a Paschate, et fetuum decimis ad Pentecosten, et frugum terrae ad omnium sanctorum (festum), et denarii S. Petri ad Petri festum, et census ecclesiae ad Martini festum.

LV. Docemus etiam, ut sacerdotes ita populi eleemosynam distribuant, ut illis tam Deum propitium reddant, quam populum ad eleemosynas assuescant.

LVI. Docemus etiam, ut sacerdotes psalmos cantent, cum eleemosynas distribuunt, et pauperes diligenter orent, ut his pro populo intercedant sedulo.

LVII. Docemus etiam, ut sacerdotes sibi caveant ab ebrietate, et illam diligenter reprehendendo interdicant aliis hominibus.

LVIII. Docemus etiam, ut nullus sacerdos sit cerevisiarius, nec aliquo modo scurram agat secum 138.0503B| ipso, vel aliis; sed sit, sicut ordinem ejus decet, prudens et venerandus.

LIX. Docemus etiam, ut sacerdotes a juramento sedulo sibi caveant, et illud valde etiam prohibeant.

LX. Docemus etiam, ut nullus sacerdos mulierum consortium nimis amet, sed diligat legitimam suam uxorem, id est Ecclesiam suam.

LXI. Docemus etiam, ut nullus sacerdos adstet falso testimonio, neque a consiliis furum sit.

LXII. Docemus etiam, ut sacerdos nunquam ordalia visitet, aut juramenta.

LXIII. Docemus etiam, ut sacerdos contra thanum non juret in compurgatione, nisi thanus praejuraverit.

LXIV. Docemus etiam, ut sacerdos non sit venator, neque accipitrarius, neque potator, sed incumbat libris suis, sicut ordinem ipsius decet.

LXV. Docemus etiam, ut quilibet sacerdos confessionem et poenitentiam doceat eum qui ipsi confitetur, et ad emendationem quoque adjuvet, et aegroto S. Eucharistiam praebeat, cum ei opus est, et ungat illum quoque, si hoc desideret, et post obitum diligenter involvat; neque permittatur aliquid vanum circa corpus, sed cum Dei timore decenter sepeliatur.

LXVI. Docemus etiam, ut quilibet sacerdos oleum habeat tam ad baptismum, quam ad aegrotos inungendos; sit etiam paratus jus populi et Christianismum sedulo promovere quovis modo tam bene praedicando, quam bonum exemplum praebendo; tunc largietur ei Deus omnipotens quod ipsi maxime acceptum erit.

LXVII. Docemus etiam, ut quilibet sacerdos norit respondere, cum chrisma tollit, quid in orationibus pro rege et episcopo fecerit.

DE CONFESSIONE.
I. Quando aliquis voluerit confessionem facere peccatorum suorum, viriliter agat, et non erubescat confiteri scelera, et facinora se accusando; quia inde venit indulgentia, et quia sine confessione nulla est venia. Confessio enim sanat, confessio justificat.

Magna hic lacuna, sive spatium in ms. codice, cui caetera alias inserturus videbatur scriba.

Praeveniat hunc famulum tuum, quaeso, Domine, misericordia tua, ut omnes iniquitates ejus celeri indulgentia deleantur per Jesum Christum Dominum nostrum.

Exaudi, quaeso, Domine, supplicum preces clamantium ad te, quaeso, Domine.

II. Quicunque est medicus animarum hominum et earum actiones norit, studeat divisionem et discrimen, quomodo hominum actionibus poenitentiam injungat; attamen non condemnet eos, neque desperare faciat. Cum homo delicta sua ei confiteri vult, exaudiat eum primo patienter, quam prudens ipsius sit intentio; si velit et possit humiliter actiones suas confiteri, et tu percipias, quod poeniteat peccatorum suorum, doce ipsum amanter et cum misericordia. Si non possit actiones suas confiteri et reatus suos examinare,

III. Interroga eum de moribus ipsius, et extorque reatus illius, et expone actiones ejus, et cogita quod nunquam debeas eodem modo judicare divites et pauperes, liberos et servos, senes et juvenes, sanos et infirmos, humiles et superbos, fortes et debiles, sacris initiatos et laicos.

Quodlibet factum judex prudens discernere debet prudenter, quando factum sit, et ubi, vel quando; nullo tempore injustum permissum est, attamen quis diebus festis et jejuniis et locis festivis quam diligentissime ab eo sibi caveat. Et quanto potentioris et majoris ordinis homo sit, tanto gravius coram Deo et coram mundo injustitiam emendare debet, quoniam potens et impotens non possunt aequalia onera habere, nec infirmus firmo similis esse; hi ergo sunt distinguendi et discrete discernendi.

IV. Posthaec surgat humiliter ad confessorem suum, et dicat primo: Ego credo in Dominum, summum Patrem, omnium rerum gubernatorem, et in Filium, et in Spiritum sanctum; et ego credo vivere post mortem; et ego credo resurgere in die judicii, et omne hoc credo per Dei potentiam et misericordiam ejus mereri.

V. Et tunc dicat animo poenitenti et humili confessionem suam confessario suo, inclinans humiliter, et sic dicat:
Ego confiteor omnipotenti Deo, et confessario meo, spirituali medico, omnia peccata mea, quibus per malignitatem spiritus unquam pollutus fui, sive in factis, sive in cogitationibus, sive cum masculis, sive cum feminis, vel cum aliqua creatura, peccata naturalia sive praeternaturalia.

VI. Confiteor gastrimargiam ciborum tam mane quam vespere. Confiteor omnem avaritiam, et invidiam, et detractionem, et bilingue vitium, mendacium, et injustam gloriam, et vaniloquium, et injustam magnificentiam, et omnem superbiam, quae ad corporis mei pravum consilium accidit. Confiteor quod nimis saepe fuerim peccati auctor, et peccati fautor, et peccati conscius, et peccati doctor.

VII. Confiteor animi mei homicidium, et perjuria, et seditionem, et superbiam, neglectum praeceptum Dei. Confiteor omnia, quae unquam oculis vidi ad avaritiam vel ad detractionem, vel auribus ad inutilia audivi, vel ore meo vana locutus sum.

VIII. Confiteor omnia corporis mei peccata, cutis, et carnis, et opis, et nervorum, et renum, et cartilaginum, et linguae, et labiorum, et faucium, et dentium, et comae et medullae, et rei cujusque mollis vel durae, humidae vel siccae. Confiteor quod baptisma meum pejus servaverim quam Domino meo sum pollicitus et ordinem meum, quem in amorem Dei et sanctorum ipsius debebam custodire, et in meam ipsius aeternam salutem ego non custodivi debito modo. Confiteor quod horas meas canonicas saepius neglexerim, et pejeraverim in dominorum meorum animam, et Domini mei nomen in vanum sumpserim.

IX. Omnium (peccatorum) rogo a Domino meo remissionem ut nunquam diabolus mihi insidietur, ut absque confessione et emendatione peccatorum meorum (non moriar), sicut hodie confiteor omnes meos reatus coram Domino Salvatore Christo, qui gubernat coelum et terram, et coram hoc sancto altari, et his reliquiis, et coram confessario meo, et Domini presbytero, et sum in pura et in vera confessione, et in bona voluntate omnia mea peccata emendare, et deinde taliter abstinere, qualiter unquam possim.

X. Et tu, Salvator Christe, sis misericors animae meae, et remitte ac dele peccata mea, et reatus meos, quae olim vel unquam antea commisi, et duc me ad sublime tuum regnum, et ibi habitem cum sanctis tuis et electis absque fine in aeternum. Jam te oro humiliter, sacerdos Domini, ut sis testis meus in die judicii, ut diabolus nequeat in me potestatem habere. et ut tu apud Dominum sis advocatus meus, quod peccata mea et reatus meos emendem, et ab aliis hujusmodi abstineam: ad hoc adjuvet me Dominus, qui vivit et regnat in aeternum. Amen.

MODUS IMPONENDI POENITENTIAM.

I. Senex et juvenis, dives et pauper, sanus et infirmus, et cujuscunque ordinis, et si quis aliquid invitus peccaverit, non sit similis ei qui voluntarie et sponte de industria peccavit; et si quis etiam necessitate coactus deliquerit, sit protectione et correctione legis semper dignus, quia necessitate coactus erat ad id quod perpetravit.

II. Quodlibet factum distinguendum est caute coram Deo et coram mundo.

Hi ritus observantur trans mare, hoc est:

III. Ut quilibet episcopus sit in sede sua episcopali die Mercurii, quem appellamus caput jejunii; tunc quilibet illorum, qui peccatis mortalibus pollutus est, in illa provincia ad eum veniat illo die, et peccata sua ei fateatur, et ille tunc doceat eum poenitentiam, juxta quamlibet reatus rationem; qui si magnae sit enormitatis, removeatur ab ecclesiastica communione, attamen ad propriam necessitatem excitetur, et admoneatur, et ipse sic cum venia ejus domum revertatur.

IV. Et inde die Jovis ante Pascha omnes ad suum quilibet locum congregentur, et cantet super eum episcopus, et absolutionem det; et ille sic postea domum revertatur cum episcopi benedictione: hoc ita observandum est ab omni Christianorum populo.

V. Attamen sacerdos diligenter considerare debet, quali cum contritione, et quali cum perfectione poenitentiam, quae ipsi imposita erat, compensaverit, et quomodo ipsi remissionem dare debeat.

VI. Si laicus alium occidat sine causa, jejunet VII annos, III pane et aqua, IV, sicuti confessarius eum docuerit, et post septem annos compenset; postea diligenter lugeat delictum suum, qua poterit industria, quoniam incognitum est quomodo accipiatur poenitentia ejus apud Deum.

VII. Si quis alterum occidere velit, et nequeat voluntatem suam implere, jejunet tres annos, unum pane et aqua, et duos sicuti confessarius ipsius eum docuerit.

VIII. Si laicus invitus aliquem occidat, jejunet tres annos; unum pane et aqua, et duos sicut confessarius illius eum docuerit, et lugeat delictum suum semper.

IX. Si sit subdiaconus, jejunet sex annos. Si sit diaconus, jejunet septem annos. Si sit sacerdos, jejunet decem annos, et episcopus XII, et lugeat semper.

X. Si quis infantem suum occiderit invitus, jejunet quinque annos, tres pane et aqua, ut supra.

XI. Si episcopus vel sacerdos aliquem occiderit, perdat ordinem suum, et postea diligenter compenset.

XII. Si uxor infantem suum enecet intra se, vel postquam natus sit, potu vel aliis rebus, jejunet decem annos, tres pane et aqua, et septem prouti confessarius ejus ex misericordia ei sanciverit, et deinde illud lugeat.

XIII. Si quis mancipium suum occiderit, sine culpa in furore suo, jejunet tres annos.

XIV. Si mulier maritum suum verberet ex aliqua zelotypia, et ille inde moriatur, et ille sit innocens, jejunet septem annos, et si ille sit reus, jejunet tres annos, et lugeat dilectum suum semper.

XV. Si quis seipsum sponte occidat armis, vel aliqua diaboli instigatione, non est permissum ut pro tali homine missae cantentur, neque cum aliquo psalmi cantu corpus terrae inferatur, neque in pura sepultura jaceat sepultus. Illud idem judicium faciendum est ei, qui pro reatu suo vitam suam tormentis finit, quales sunt fur, homicida et domini proditor.

XVI. Si quis se cum bestia polluit, vel masculus cum alio, si sit XX annorum, jejunet quindecim annos; et si vir uxorem suam habeat, et ipse 40 annos natus sit, et tale quid committat, abstineat, et jejunet quandiu in vivis est, et non praesumat Domini corpus percipere, antequam mors illum avocet. Juvenis et insipiens acriter verberetur, qui tale quid commiserit.

XVII. Si quis adulterium committit, per septennium tribus diebus in hebdomada jejunet pane et aqua, sive sit uxor, sive maritus.

XVIII. Si quis conjugem suam deserit, et ducit aliam uxorem, adulterium committit, non concedatur ei aliquid eorum jurium, quae ad Christianos pertinent, nec mortuo, nec vivo, nec sepeliatur homo hic cum Christianis. Et idem etiam uxori fiat. Et cognatorum, qui idem fecerint, perdat quilibet jus suum, nisi citius reverti et sedulo corrigere velint.

XIX. Si quis habeat uxorem et concubinam etiam, nullus sacerdos ei ullum aliquod officium praestet cum Christianis, nisi ad emendationem revertatur, unam retineat sibi sive uxorem, sive concubinam.

XX. Si vir cum alterius legitima uxore coeat, vel uxor cum alterius uxoris legitimo conjuge, jejunet septem annos, tres pane et aqua, et quatuor sicut confessarius eum docuerit, et lugeat delictum suum semper.

XXI. Si quae uxor duos fratres in conjugium sumat, unum post alium, judicio obnoxii sunt illi, et seduli in poenitentia sint quandiu vivunt, prout confessarius eorum docuerit ipsos; et in eorum obitu sacerdos faciat iis officium, sicut Christianis fit, si promiserint se melius emendare voluisse, si diutius vixissent.

XXII. Si quis in aliquo nefando peccati consortio permanserit, usquedum vitam suam finiat absque ulla resipiscentia; non novimus aliquod ei consilium suppeditare, nisi quod hoc ad Dei judicium pertineat, neque potest absolvi.

XXIII. Si uxor aliqua desponsata sit, non sit permissum ut aliquis alius vir eam illi eripiat; si quis hoc fecerit, sit excommunicatus.

XXIV. Si quis cum fraude sua uxorem vel virginem invitam rapuerit ad illicitum concubitum, sit ille excommunicatus.

XXV. Si quis illecebris suis alterius hominis pedissequam ab eo seducat scortationis causa, et cum illa invita coeat; si sit sacris initiatus homo, perdat ordinem suum; si sit laicus, sit excommunicatus ab omnibus Christianis officiis.

XXVI. Si quae virgo desponsata est, et hoc temporis intervallo abducatur, vel sub aliquo praetextu auferatur ab eo cui desponsata erat, et deinde accidat ut illa in conspectum ejus veniat, cum venia illi possunt coire, quoniam contra voluntatem suam illa ab eo aberat.

XXVII. Si femina consecrata sit, et deinde ad mundanam vanitatem revertatur, et familiam alat, et cogitet se ex possessione sua emendaturam esse quod a Deo declinaverit, hoc nihil est; sed deserat peccati consortium, et revertatur ad Christum, et vitam suam vivat, sicut confessarius illius docuerit, et diligentissime deinde delictum corrigat.

XXVIII. Si presbyter vel monachus hominem occiderit, perdat ordinem suum, et jejunet decem annos; quinque pane et aqua, et quinque tribus diebus per hebdomadam; et reliquis fruatur cibo suo, et lugeat delictum suum semper.
Diaconus octo pane et aqua, et reliquis ut supra.
Clericus IV annos; VI pane et aqua.
Laicus V annos; III pane et aqua, ut supra.

XXIX.
Si quis sacris initiatum occiderit, vel proprium proximum cognatum, deserat terram et possessionem suam, et faciat sicuti papa instruxerit eum, et lugeat semper.

XXX. Si presbyter vel monachus concubitum lascivum exerceat, vel conjugium violet, jejunet X annos, et lugeat semper. Diaconus VII, clericus VI, Laicus V [annis] ut propter homicidium.

XXXI. Si presbyter vel monachus vel diaconus legitimam uxorem habet, antequam consecratus sit, eam deserat et ordines recipiat, et postea propter concubitum illam saepe recipiat, jejunet quilibet eorum tanquam pro homicidio, et valde lugeant.
XXXII. Si sacerdos, vel monachus vel diaconus vel laicus vel clericus cum monacha coeat, jejunet quilibet, prouti ordini suo convenit tanquam pro homicidio, et semper a carne abstineat; et monialis decem annos, uti etiam sacerdos, et lugeant semper.

XXXIII. Si quis cum moniali coire vellet, et ipsa nollet, jejunet unum annum pro injusta illa voluntate pane et aqua. Si quis vellet coire cum alterius legitima uxore, et ipsa nollet, jejunet unum annum pro injusta illa voluntate pane et aqua.

XXXIV. Si quis coire vellet cum alterius legitima conjuge, et ipsa nollet, jejunet tres quadragesimas pane et aqua, unam in aestate, aliam in autumno, tertiam in hieme.

XXXV. Si quis velit cum uxore injuste coire, jejunet XL dies pane et aqua.

XXXVI. Si quis alium cum filia sua deprehendat, compenset apud [puellae] amicos, et uterque jejunet unum annum diebus Mercurii et Veneris quandiu vixerit, et lugeat semper delictum suum.

XXXVII. Si quis cum bestia coeat, jejunet XV annos; octo pane et aqua, et septem alios quolibet anno tribus diebus quadragesimis, et diebus Mercurii et Veneris, quandiu vixerit, et lugeat semper delictum suum.

XXXVIII. Si quis seipsum propria de voluntate polluat, jejunet tribus annis; quolibet tribus quadragesimis pane et aqua, et abstineat a carne singulis diebus, excepto die Solis.

XXXIX. Si quis alium veneficio occidat, jejunet septem annos, tres pane et aqua, et quatuor alios annos tribus diebus per hebdomadam pane et aqua; et lugeat semper.

XL. Si quis homini paxillum infigat, jejunet tres annos; unum pane et aqua, et duos tribus diebus per hebdomadam pane et aqua; et si homo propter paxillum illum moriatur, tunc jejunet septem annis; sicuti hic ascriptum est, et lugeat delictum suum semper.

XLI. Si quis veneficio utatur ad alterius amorem (sibi conciliandum) et ei (illud) det in esu vel in potu, vel in arte incantandi, si sit laicus, jejunet dimidium anni diebus Mercurii et Veneris pane et aqua, et aliis diebus utatur cibo suo, excepta carne. Clericus unum annum, ut supra, tribus diebus per hebdomadam pane et aqua. Diaconus tres annos, ut supra. Presbyter quinque annos; unum eorum pane et aqua, et quatuor quolibet die Veneris pane et aqua, et aliis diebus abstineat a carne.

XLII. Si quis turpiter in praeternaturalibus rebus contra Dei creaturam per aliquam rem se polluerit ipsum, lugeat semper quandiu vixerit, juxta illud quod factum est.

XLIII. Si quis in somno infantem suum comprimat, ut moriatur, jejunet tres annos; unum pane et aqua, et biennium tribus diebus per hebdomadem; et si per ebrietatem factus sit, compenset gravius, sicut confessarius ipsius docuerit, et lugeat illud semper.

XLIV. Si infirmus infans ethnicus (id est absque baptismo) decedat, et hoc ex sacerdotis procrastinatione sit, perdat ordinem suum, et sedulo hoc corrigat; et si id per negligentiam amicorum fiat, jejunent tres annos, unum pane et aqua, et biennium tribus diebus per septimanam, et lugeant hoc semper.

XLV. Si quis Christianum ad ethnicismum vendat, non sit dignus aliqua requie cum Christianis, nisi ipsum deinde domum redemerit, quem antea vendiderat foris; et si hoc facere nequit, dividatur pretium illud totum, Dei gratia, et alium redimat alio pretio, et eum tunc dimittat, et ad haec augeat compensationem tres annos integros, sicuti confessarius illum docuerit. Et si pecuniam non habeat qua hominem redimere posset, compenset gravius, hoc est, septem annos integros, et lugeat semper.

XLVI. Si quis seipsum valde labefactet multifariis peccatis, et ille deinde ab eis abstinere et sedulo corrigere velit, inclinet ad monasterium, et serviat ibi semper Deo et hominibus, sicuti docetur, vel a patria longe peregrinetur, et poenitentiam agat semper, quandiu vixerit, atque salutem quaerat animae suae saltem in terra per gravissimam compensationem, quam unquam experiri possit, prouti docetur.

DE POENITENTIA.

I. In hac confessione valde conducit alicujus theologi necessarium auxilium, sicuti omnino bonus medicus est aegroti hominis medela.

II. Per concupiscentiam homo saepe peccat, et haud raro per diaboli instigationem; et hoc est terribile, quod sacris initiati tam graviter apud Deum peccent, ut ordinem amittant.

III. Et ad hoc corrigendum opus est rigida poenitentia, semper tamen juxta ordinis et juxta peccati modum, secundum leges canonicas. Et etiam quaerendum est de hominis viribus, et de [satisfactionis] ejus modo, et de ipsiusmet animi compunctione. Aliqui poenitentiam agant annum; aliqui plus anno; et deinde pro delicti modo, aliqui poeniteant mensem, aliqui plus mense; aliqui septimanam poeniteant, aliqui plus septimana; aliqui diem poeniteant, et aliqui plus die, et aliqui omnes vitae suae dies.

IV. Si medicus gravia vulnera bene curare debet, adhibeat oportet bona medicamenta; nulla vulnera sunt adeo mala quam vulnera peccati, quoniam iis homo meretur aeternam mortem, nisi per confessionem, et per abstinentiam, et per poenitentiam sanetur.

V. Tunc medicus debet esse sapiens et prudens, qui vulnera curare debet. Per bonam doctrinam prius curetur, et hoc facto expurgetur venenum quod in eo est, hoc est, ut seipsum prius purget per confessionem.

VI. Omnis homo evomere debet peccata per bonam doctrinam cum confessione, eodem modo ac fit lethalis morbus per bonam potionem.

VII. Non potest aliquis medicus bene curare antequam venenum excesserit, neque homo aliquis etiam poenitentiam bene docere potest eum, qui confiteri nolit, neque aliquis homo peccata absque confessione corrigere potest; sicut minus bene curari potest qui lethale quid exhausit, nisi venenum omnino evomat.

VIII. Post confessionem per poenitentiam quis Dei misericordiam potest cito mereri, si cum interiori corde plangat, et lugeat quod per diaboli instigationem antea seductus sit ad injustitiam.

IX. Prudentem confessarium valde etiam decet prudens poenitentia, sicut omnino boni medici est aegrum hominem curare. De compensatione necessarii usus et de operibus hominis inquiri debet secundum leges canonicas, et ratio statui etiam pro viribus, et pro modo, et pro eo, qui agnoscit cordis sui luctum et sollicitudinem propriam

X. Gravis poenitentia est, quod laicus arma sua deponat, et nudus pedibus longe peregrinetur, et non pernoctetur alicubi, et jejunet et valde vigilet, et oret diligenter die ac nocte, et volens se fatiget, et ita incultus sit, ut ferro nec crines nec ungues tangat.

XI. Nec ut ingrediatur thermas, nec lectum mollem, nec gustet carnem, nec aliquid ejus unde ebrius esse possit; non ingrediatur ecclesias, attamen locum sanctum diligenter quaerat, et reatum suum confiteatur, et intercessionem roget; et neminem osculetur, sed semper peccata sua valde lugeat.

XII. Crudeliter agit qui seipsum hoc modo damnat, attamen beatus est ille, si nulli alii rei invigilet, quam ut plene (peccata) corrigat; quoniam nullus homo in mundo adeo valde Deum peccatis offendit, quin apud Deum emendare queat, si hoc sedulo aggrediatur.

XIII. Poenitentiae fiunt variis modis, et multi homines eleemosynis (eam) redimere possunt.

XIV. Si quis ad hoc facultates habeat, erigat ecclesiam in laudem Dei; et si praeterea valeat, adjiciat terram, et admittat decem juniores, qui ibi pro eo servire, et ibi quotidie Deo possint ministrare; et instauret etiam Dei ecclesiam ubique pro facultate sua, et instauret vias publicas pontibus super aquas profundans, et super coenosas vias, et distribuat, Dei causa, diligenter id quod habet juxta facultatum suarum rationem, et adjuvet diligenter pauperes, viduas, et orphanos et peregrinos; manumittat servos suos proprios, et redimat ab aliis hominibus servorum suorum libertatem, ac saltem pauperes bello vastatos, et pascatur egenos, et vestiat hospitio, et foco, balneo, et lectis eos prospiciat, et in sui ipsius necessitatem ubique diligenter intercessionem faciat in missarum et psalmorum cantibus, et semetipsum ex devotione erga Dominum suum castiget quam acerrime per abstinentiam a cibo et potu, et quacunque corporali concupiscentia.

XV. Et si quis autem minus facultatum habeat, diligenter pro viribus suis faciat quod potest; decimet in Dei timore omne quod habet, et examinet seipsum, quoties opportune poterit, et saepe visitet cum eleemosynis suis ecclesias, et sanctificet locum cum salutatione candelari, et concedat hospitium, et cibum, et protectionem eis quibus opus est, et ignem ac alimentum, et lectum ac balneum, et faciat vestiri et adjuvari pauperes quantum potest.

XVI. Visitet ex amore Dei aegros animo, et aegrotos, ac mortuos sepeliat ex devotione erga Deum, et ipse in occultis locis in genua provolvatur saepe, et super terram totam se prosternat saepe ac crebro, et jejunet ac vigilet, et diligenter oret die et nocte saepe ac crebro. Et si quis minus adhuc minus facultatum habeat, pro viribus suis faciat sedulo quidquid potest, saltem labore conterat corpus suum adversus libidinem. Si prius per mollem libidinem diabolo placuerit, jejunet nunc, econtrario, quod id prius per injustam ingluviem perpetraverat; vigilet et laboret contrario, quod prius saepe somnolentus et piger fuerit, cum non deberet, vel inutiliter nimis V gilaverit; sustineat frigus et balneum frigidum contra aestum, quem per cupidinem suam ubique excitavit. Et si aliquem ubique injuste sponte exacerbaverit, compenset diligenter; et si aliquis eum offendat, libenter remittat ex timore Dei, et semper, quantum poterit, cogitet diligentissime quidquid compensationis loco facere possit contra singula peccata, quae per diaboli semen prius adoleverant; et si de via aliquem ad lucrandum quidquam deduxerit, ducat eum diligenter postea in rectam viam. Hoc est quod ego volo; si aliquem ad peccatum incitaverit, faciat ei sicut necessarium est, deducat eum inde, et ducat illum in rectam viam et quemlibet diligenter dehortetur a peccatis; tunc statim peccata ipsius erunt leviora.

XVII. Idem judicium potest quis cum confessarii consilio sibi ipsi judicare, qui constanter a peccatis suis abstinere, et peccata sua corrigere vult, distribuat ex devotione erga Deum omne quod habet, et deserat cum iis totam terram et patriam, et omnem mundi amorem, et serviat Domino suo die et nocte, et laboret quam maxime potest contra propriam cupidinem omnes vitae suae dies. Quid amplius facere potest, quam ut hortetur (proprii commodi causa) quemlibet hominem ad jus, quam potest diligentissime.

Hic indicitur quomodo aegrotus jejunium suum redimere debet.

XVIII. Unius diei jejunium uno denario redimi potest: quilibet homo potest unius diei jejunium redimere ducentis et viginti psalmis; quilibet homo XII mensium jejunium redimere potest 30 solidis, vel si aliquem (e carcere) liberet, qui tanti aestimetur. Et pro unius diei jejunio, ut cantetur sex vicibus: Beati immacul. et sex vicibus Pater noster et pro unius diei jejunio, ut genua flectantur, et incurventur LX vicibus ad terram cum Pater noster. Potest etiam aliquis unius diei jejunium redimere, si omnia membra extendat ad Deum in orationibus suis, et cum vera contritione, et cum fide recta, et XV vicibus cantet Miserere mei, Deus, et XV vicibus Pater noster. Et tunc ei concessa sit potius diei allevatio peccatorum.

XIX. Septennale jejunium quis XII mensibus compensare potest, si quotidie cantando finiat psalterii psalmos, et itidem nocte, et I vespere. Redimi potest etiam per unam missam XII dierum jejunium; et per decem missas allevari potest IV mensium jejunium, et per 30 missas allevari potest XII mensium jejunium, si velit ex vero Dei amore pro seipso intercedere, et peccata sua confessario suo confiteri, et eadem corrigere, prout ille eum docuerit, et diligenter semper ab iis abstinere.

DE MAGNATIBUS.

I. Ita vir potens et amicorum dives poenitentiam suam auxilio amicorum multum allevare potest. Primo in Dei nomine per confessarii sui testimonium ostendat veram fidem, et condonet omnibus illis qui erga eum peccaverunt, et faciat confessionem suam intrepide, et polliceatur abstinentiam, et suscipiat poenitentiam cum multo gemitu.

II. Deponat tunc arma sua et inanem vestium cultum, et sumat scipionem in manus, et eat sedulo nudus pedibus, et corpori induat lanea, vel cilicia, et non ingrediatur lectum, sed jaceat in area, et faciat, ut VII annorum numerus intra tres dies ita temperetur; primo accipiat in auxilium sibi 12 homines, et jejunent tres dies pane et viridibus oleribus, et aqua, et conquirat sibi ad consummandum illud, quomodocumque potest, septies 120 homines, qui jejunent singuli pro eo tribus diebus; tunc jejunantur tot jejunia quot sunt dies in VII annis.

III. Cum quis jejunat, distribuat fercula, quibus ipse uti deberet, omnibus Dei pauperibus, et tribus diebus, quibus jejunat, negligat mundi negotia, et die ac nocte quam saepissime potest in ecclesiis habitet, et ibi cum eleemosynario lumine vigilet diligenter, et ad Deum clamet, et remissionem petat animo gementi, et saepe genua flectat super crucis signum; interdum erigat se, interdum se prosternat, et diligenter noscat vir potens lacrymas fundere, et peccata deflere. Et pascat tribus diebus pauperes quotquot maxime potest, et quarto die abluat omnes, et hospitio excipiat, et pecuniam donet, et ipse poenitentiam agens sit circa lotionem pedum eorum (occupatus), et missae dicantur eo die pro ipso tot quot unquam obtineri possunt, et illarum missarum tempore detur ei absolutio, et tum sanctam Eucharistiam percipiat, nisi nimium gravis sit peccator, ut adhuc (eam percipere) nequeat: et tunc polliceatur saltem quod semper abhinc Dei voluntatem peragere velit, et ab omni injustitia per Dei auxilium imposterum abstinere, Christianismum quam strenue unquam potest, juste tenere, et omnem gentilismum omnino abjicere, animum et mores, verba et opera sedulo corrigere, omnem justitiam colere, et injustitiam evitare per Dei auxilium, quam diligentissime unquam possit. Et maximo suo commodo faciet ille, qui hoc praestiterit, quod Deo pollicitus erat.

IV. Haec est potentis viri et amicorum divitis poenitentiae allevatio; ast infirmus non potest ita procedere, sed debet in seipso illud exquirere diligentius. Et hoc est etiam aequissimum, ut quilibet propria sua delicta diligenti correctione ulciscatur in seipso: Scriptum est enim « Quia unusquisque onus suum portabit. »

LEGES ECCLESIASTICAE REGIS EDGARI.(Ex ms. coll. Corp. Chr. Cantabr. § 28 et k. 2.)
EADGARI LEGES.
Hoc est institutum quod Eadgarus cum sapientum suorum consilio instituit in gloriam Dei, et sibi ipsi in dignitatem regiam, et in utilitatem omni populo suo.

I. De immunitate ecclesiae, et debitis eidem reddendis.

Hoc sit igitur primum quod ecclesiae Dei jure suo dignae sint, et dentur omnes decimae primariae ecclesiae ad quam parochia pertinet; et tunc praestetur sive de terra thani, sive de terra villanorum, prouti aratrum circumducitur.

II. De censu ecclesiastico.

Si quis thanorum sit qui in feodo suo ecclesiam habet, in qua sit coemeterium, det tunc tertiam partem propriarum decimarum suarum ecclesiae suae. Si quis ecclesiam habet in qua non sit coemeterium, tunc ex novem partibus presbytero suo det quidquid velit, et transeat quilibet ecclesiasticus census ad primariam ecclesiam de qualibet terra libera.

III. De decimis.

Et singulae fetuum decimae praestentur ad Pentecosten, et terrae frugum ad aequinoctium. Et quilibet census ecclesiasticus praestetur ad festum Martini, per plenam mulctam, quamlibet judicialis adnotat. Et si quis decimam praestare nolit, sicuti diximus, proficiscatur ad eum. Praefectus regis, et episcopi, et ecclesiae presbyter, et sumant, invito eo, decimam partem, quae ad ecclesiam pertinet, et assignent ei nonam partem, et dividantur octo partes in duo, et capiat dominus dimidium, dimidium episcopus, sive sit regis sive thani minister.

IV. De nummo in singulas domos imposito.

Et quilibet nummus in domos singulas impositus, detur ad Petri festum diem, et qui ad illum terminum (eum) non solverit, portet eum Romam, et alios praeterea 30 denarios, et referat inde testimonium quod ibi tot tradiderit. Et tunc domum reversus, solvat regi 120 solidos, et si eum iterum solvere nolit, portet illum deinde Romam, et simile quid compenset, et tunc domum reversus, solvat regi ducentos solidos. Si tertia vice reddere nolit, perdat omne quod habet.

V. De festis diebus et jejuniis.

Quodlibet diei solis festum celebretur ab hora pomeridiana diei Saturni, usque ad diluculum diei lunae, sub mulcta quam liber judicialis adnotat; et singuli alii festi dies (celebrentur) sicut justum est. Et institutum jejunium servetur cum omni devotione.

The Scriptorium Project is the work of a small group of lay people of various apostolic churches who are interested in the preservation, transmission, and translation of the works of the early and medieval church. Our efforts are to make the works of the church fathers accessible to anyone who might have an interest in Christian antiquities and the theological, philosophical, and moral writings that have become the bedrock of Western Civilization.

To-date, our releases have pulled from the Greek, Syriac, Georgian, Latin, Celtic, Ethiopian, and Coptic traditions of Christianity, and have been pulled from sundry local traditions and languages.

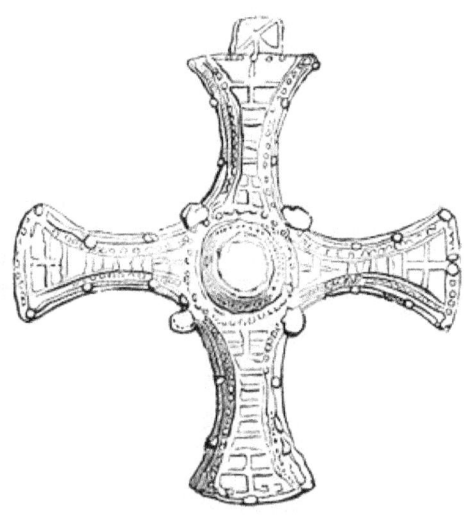

Other Selections from the Early Anglo-Saxon Church Series:

Church Laws by Alfred the Great, King of Anglo-Saxons (May 2006)
Church Laws by Guthram, King of East Anglia (Feb. 2007)
Two Works by St. Dunstan of Canterbury (Jan. 2008)
The Eight Principal Vices by St. Aldheim of Malmesbury (May 2013)
For the Catholic Easter and the Roman Tonsure by Ceolfridus of Wiremouth (June 2013)
Penitential (Poenitentiale) by Theodore of Tarsus (July 2013)
Life of St. Augustine of Canterbury by Goscelin of Saint-Bertin (Aug. 2013)
The English Calendar by St. Bede the Venerable (Nov. 2015)
Letter to King Aethelred by Pope John VII (Dec. 2015)
The Life of the Christian by Fastidius of Britain (Apr. 2017)
Privileges of the Abbot of Cantergury by St. Augustine of Canterbury (Sept. 2017)
A Song of Aethelwolf by Aethelwolf of Lindisfarne (Nov. 2017)
Decrees of Aethelbert by St. Aethelbert, King of Kent (Feb. 2019)
Donations by St. Aethelbert, King of Kent (May 2020)
Life of St. Augustine of Canterbury by Goscelin of Saint-Bertin (Dec. 2020)

Canons of the Council of London by Edgar, King of the English (Dec. 2023)

www.ingramcontent.com/pod-product-compliance
Lightning Source LLC
LaVergne TN
LVHW052004060526
838201LV00059B/3835